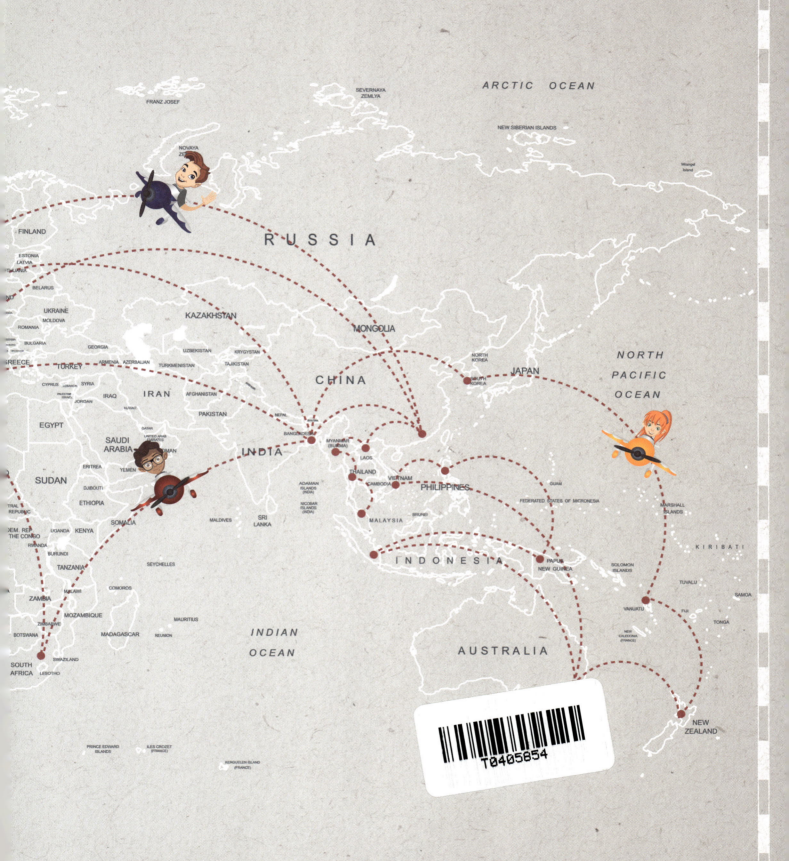

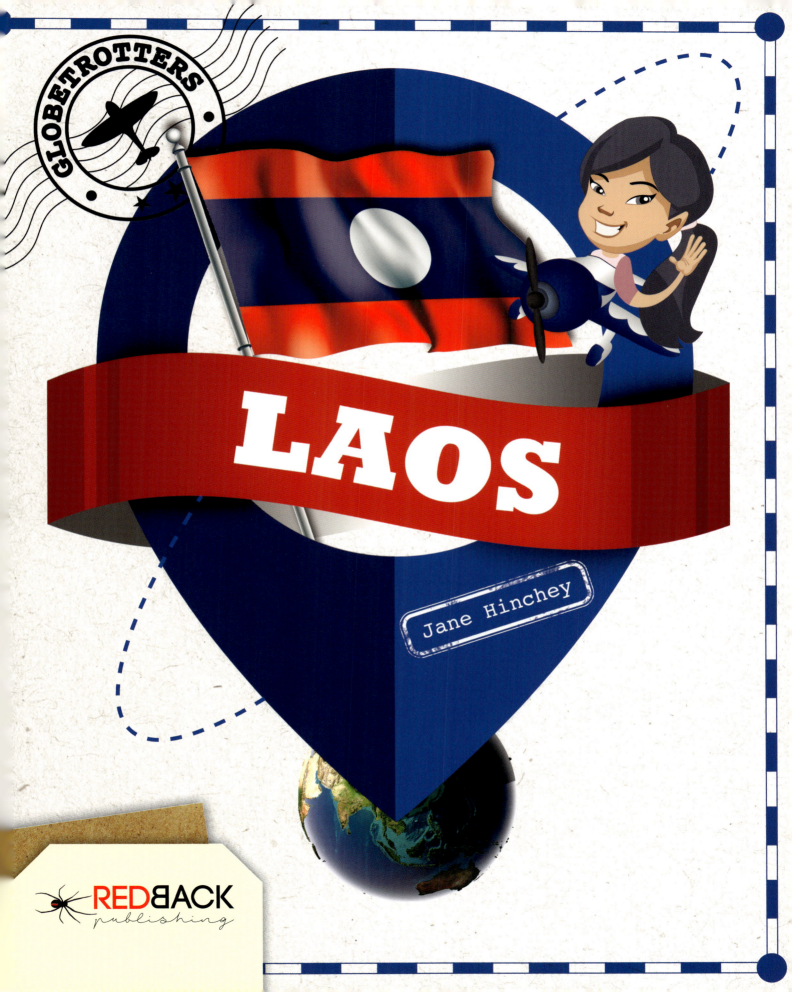

First Published 2022 by
Redback Publishing
PO Box 357 Frenchs Forest NSW 2086
Australia

www.redbackpublishing.com
orders@redbackpublishing.com

© Redback Publishing 2022

ISBN 978-1-922322-28-9 HBK

All rights reserved. No part of this publication may be reproduced in anyform or by any means (including photocopying or storing it in any medium by electronic means and whether or not transiently or incidentally to some other use of this publication) without the written permission of the copyright owner. Applications for the copyright owner's written permission should be addressed to the publisher.

Author: Jane Hinchey
Editor: Marlene Vaughan
Design: Redback Publishing

Original illustrations © Redback Publishing 2022
Originated by Redback Publishing

Printed and bound in Malaysia

Acknowledgements
Abbreviations: l—left, r—right, b—bottom, t—top, c—centre, m—middle
We would like to thank the following for permission to reproduce photographs: (Images © shutterstock) p6tl Yurii Vasyliev / Shutterstock.com, p7ml Paolo Arsie Pelanda / Shutterstock.com, p10b PStephane Bidouze / Shutterstock.com, p11br demamiel62 / Shutterstock.com, p12tr PixHound / Shutterstock.com, p12ml Stefano Ember / Shutterstock.com, p15bl Shahjehan / Shutterstock.com, p16ml Suthikait Teerawattanaphan / Shutterstock.com, p19tr i viewfinder / Shutterstock.com, p20br Sambulov Yevgeniy / Shutterstock.com, p21mr kalapangha / Shutterstock.com, p21bl KaikeoSaiyasane / Shutterstock.com, p24bl Huy Thoai / Shutterstock.com, p25tl jaume/Shutterstock.com, p27ml by Karen Stout Via Wikimedia, p28br mundosemfim / Shutterstock.com

Disclaimer
Every effort has been made to contact copyright holders of any material reproduced in this book. Any omissions will be rectified in subsequent printings if notice is given to the publisher.

A catalogue record for this book is available from the National Library of Australia

CONTENTS

Map of Laos 4
Welcome to Laos 6
At a Glance 7
The Most Heavily Bombed Country in the World 8
People 10
Daily Life 11
The Arts 12
Clothes 13
Language 14
Education 15
Life in Cities 16
Life in Rural Areas 17
History Timeline 18
Religion 20
Food 22
Geography and Climate 24
Fabulous Flora and Fauna 26
Major Sights 28
Transport 30
Flags, Symbols and Emblems 31
Glossary and Index 32

MAP OF LAOS

Kuang Si Falls
LUANG PRABANG

VIENTIANE

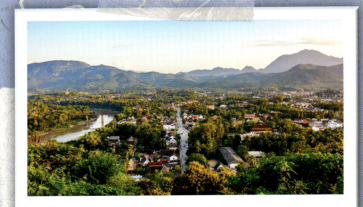

LUANG PRABANG

VANG VIENG

Pha That Luang
VIENTIANE

Tad Fane Waterfall
DONG HUA SAO NATIONAL PARK

Fun Fact
Laos is home to the Khone Phapheng, Southeast Asia's largest waterfall.

Kong Lor Cave
PHU HIN BUN NATIONAL PARK

Fun Fact
The oldest human fossil in Southeast Asia was found in a cave in North Laos.

SNAPSHOT

COUNTRY
Lao People's Democratic Republic

CAPITAL
Vientiane

RELIGION
Theravada Buddhism

AREA
236,800 square kilometres

POPULATION
7,389,060 (2021)

OFFICIAL LANGUAGE
Lao (official), Hmong, Khmu, French

CURRENCY	Kip
HIGHEST POINT	Phou Bia 2,820 metres

Vat Phou
CHAMPASAK PROVINCE

4000 Islands region
CHAMPASAK PROVINCE

WELCOME TO LAOS

Laos is a landlocked country in Southeast Asia, bordered by Myanmar to the northwest, Cambodia and Vietnam to the east, Thailand to the west and China to the north. Despite having no coast, Laos consists of more water than land.

Laos is a one-party socialist republic. The Lao People's Revolutionary Party (LPRP) is the only legal political party. The head of government is the Prime Minister, who is elected by a National Assembly for a five-year term.

Laos is a poor country, with approximately 18 per cent of its population living under the national poverty line. It depends on millions of dollars in aid annually.

1. Myanmar
2. Thailand
3. Cambodia
4. Vietnam
5. China

AT A GLANCE

Major Industries
Copper, tin, gold and gypsum mining, construction, garments, cement, tourism, timber, electric power and agricultural processing.

Main Agriculture
Sweet potatoes, vegetables, corn, coffee, sugarcane, tobacco, cotton, peanuts and rice.

Natural Resources
Tin, gold, gemstones gypsum, lead, zinc, coal, potash, iron ore and petroleum. Other resources include forests and potential hydro-electric power.

Farmers loading a sugarcane truck

Into the Future
The government opened Laos to the world in the 1990s. Tourism is now the fastest growing industry and plays a vital role in the Lao economy.

Main Exports:
Tin, copper, gold, wood products, garments, electricity and coffee.

Main Imports:
Machinery and equipment, vehicles, fuel and consumer goods

THE MOST HEAVILY BOMBED COUNTRY IN THE WORLD

Laos has heavy contamination from cluster munitions remnants. Landmines are explosive traps that detonate when they come into contact with a person or vehicle. Generally, they are scattered across an area or buried about 15 centimetres under the ground. There are 600 different types of landmines, grouped into two categories: anti-personnel landmines and anti-tank landmines. Anti-tank landmines are designed to destroy vehicles that drive over them. Anti-personnel landmines are triggered when they come into contact with a person, which has had serious ramifications for civilians.

Old anti-tank mine buried in the sand

Artificial legs of Laos bomb victims

Massive bomb crater in Laos

During the Vietnam War, the United States dropped two million tons of bombs on Laos; making it the world's most bombed country per capita ever. Millions of these bombs still litter the landscape undetonated. They often explode when accidentally struck by farmers, playing children or buffaloes. Huge areas of land remain unusable, which impacts agriculture, industry, tourism and the daily lives of the Lao people. Finding and dismantling landmines is an expensive and difficult process.

The Ottawa Convention

The Ottawa Convention, or Mine Ban Treaty, is an international treaty that stops the production and use of landmines.

PEOPLE

Laos has a population of around seven million people, making it one of the most sparsely populated countries in Asia. Two-thirds of the population live in rural areas, although urbanisation is steady. Vientiane is the largest city with over half a million people.

There are as many as 200 distinct ethnic groups in Laos, but the Laos government only recognizes four broad categories.

The biggest ethnic group in Laos is the Lao Loum, the country's lowlanders, which make up 68 per cent of the population. They arrived from South China over 4,000 years ago.

DAILY LIFE

Family is the focus of daily life and it is common for family to live with two or more generations. Most families are still involved in farming and retain traditional ways. Young people are expected to respect their elders and take care of them when they are old. The home is still the domain of the women with other work split between men and women. On rice farms, men do work such as ploughing, controlling water, sowing and reaping the crop. Women weed and carry the sheaves of rice to the threshing place. Other chores include hunting, the fetching of water and collection of forest food.

Farmers use buffaloes to plough rice fields

Life revolves around seasonal cycles and the Buddhist calendar.

Women beating the sheaves in rice fields

THE ARTS

Laos has a rich history of traditional arts influenced heavily by nearby cultures along the Mekong, as well as Buddhism and Hinduism. Regional and rural art forms include silverwork and goldwork, weaving and basket making, and wood and ivory carving.

Buddhist Monk showing younger kids how to play the big drum

Music is made using instruments such as flutes, plucked and bowed lutes, drums, cymbals and the 'khene', a wood-and-bamboo mouth organ. Most music is passed from generation to generation as part of an oral tradition.

CLOTHES

The female traditional costume is the sinh, with similarities to traditional Thai and Cambodian costume. It consists of a tube skirt made of silk, a blouse and a long embroidered sash that is draped across one shoulder. Many Laotian women still wear this daily.

The male traditional costume is a peasant pant called a salong.

cloth market to buy fabric for clothes

Both the sinh and salong come in various colours depending on where they are worn, such as a wedding, funeral or festival.

LANGUAGE

The official language is Lao, or Laotian, which has influenced the Khmer and Thai languages and vice versa. It is spoken by approximately 15 million people in Laos and Thailand. It is a tonal language. There are six tones for each word and each different tone changes the meaning of the word.

There are 86 other languages spoken in Laos, belonging to various ethnic groups. French is also spoken by many people.

Learn The Lingo

- **Maybe** — Bangthi
- **Good evening** — None lap fan dii
- **Please** — Khâluna
- **Yes** — Jao
- **Good morning** — Sabaï dii
- **No** — Baw
- **Thank You** — Khãwp Jai

EDUCATION

School is compulsory and all children supposedly attend between the ages of six and fifteen. However, the reality is more complex. Dropout rates are high and there are still many hurdles to overcome that make it difficult for children to attend school.

Some communities believe education is for boys only. In other areas children don't attend school because there is no way to get there or they have responsibilities working on family farms.

children cycling to school from the village

Sport

Soccer is the most popular sport in Laos. Other popular sports include Thai style boxing, Muay Lao, a form of unarmed martial art, and Sepak Takraw, which is a mixture of volleyball and football.

LIFE IN CITIES

Most of Laos is still rural. City life is limited to Vientiane and some smaller provincial cities. Unlike other Asian cities where people have migrated to these urban areas looking for work, in Laos it is more financially viable to live in a rural area close to a city and provide produce for the city dwellers.

The largest city is the capital, Vientiane, located on the Mekong River. Founded in 1562, it now has 600,000 inhabitants. Traditionally, people live in homes made of wood, but apartment blocks are now common.

Fresh vegetable trading in the morning market in Vientiane, Laos

Natural Disasters

The most common natural disasters to affect Laos are floods, droughts, earthquakes, cyclones and infectious disease epidemics. The impacts of these disasters are especially felt in rural areas where economic livelihoods are reliant on agriculture.

LIFE IN RURAL AREAS

About 80 per cent of Laos's population live in rural areas. Over 40 per cent of these people live in poverty.

For those in rural communities, their way of life has not changed much for generations. Families still live in traditional style homes and own farms or small businesses. Many generations live under one roof. Villages can consist of a few families or hundreds of families. Homes cluster together with rice fields surrounding the village.

Traditional Houses

Traditional homes in rural areas have wooden frames, thatched, tiled or iron roofs and walls of timber or woven bamboo. The houses are raised on stilts to help the flow of air and also protect from flooding. The area under the house is used for relaxation, to keep cool and to keep animals.

HISTORY TIMELINE

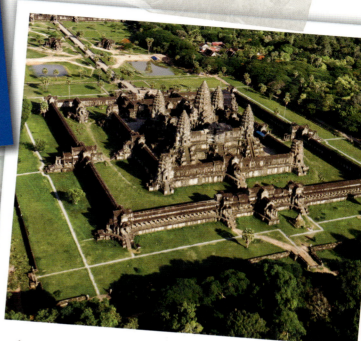

Ancient kingdom of Angkor Wat, ruled by the Khmer Empire in the 12th century

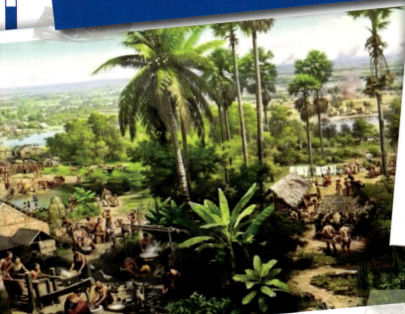

7000BC
People living in the area settle and begin farming.

900AD
The Khmer empire expands into the northern and central regions.

1560
King Setthathirath moves the capital to Vientiane.

1893
Laos becomes a French protectorate.

1945
Laos is occupied by the Japanese towards the end of World War II.

1946
French rule over Laos is resumed.

1953
Laos gains full independence a constitutional monarchy.

The Friendship Bridge over the Mekong

Statue of King Setthathirath

1960s
Laos is subjected to extensive bombing by the United States.

1975
The Pathet Lao overthrows the royalist Lao government. The Lao People's Democratic Republic is established.

1993-94
The Friendship Bridge opens across the Mekong, linking Laos and Thailand. A new age begins, opening Laos up to tourism.

2000
Laos celebrates 25 years of communist rule.

2006
Choummaly Sayasone becomes president.

2009
Rail link with Thailand opened over the Mekong at Nong Khai.

2016
Bounnhang Vorachith is appointed as president and leader of the ruling Lao People's Revolutionary Party (LPRP).

RELIGION

Laos's government recognises four religions: Buddhism, Christianity, Islam and Bahai. The Constitution provides for freedom of religion. Buddhism is the main religion in Laos, with most Lao practising Theravada Buddhism. Many young Lao men become monks for a period of time.

Animistic Paths

Many Lao people consult fortune-tellers and palmists. Astrologers are still consulted before making decisions about marriage or business and also to help choose auspicious days for major events.

Baci Ceremony

Baci is an important Lao custom where strings are tied around a person's wrist. Baci are held for both happy and sad occasions and to preserve good luck. Baci ceremonies can be held any day of the year, but elders and monks choose auspicious days on which to hold them. This ceremony has a deep meaning for Lao people and is an important part of their culture.

Songkran - the Water Splashing Festival to celebrate the Lunar New Year

Festival of Lights in Luang Prabang, Laos

Important Celebrations

There are 13 public holidays in Laos. Most festivals are Buddhist and tied to the Lunar calendar, so dates change annually. There are many other local festivals and celebrations.

FOOD

Lao cuisine is very similar to its Northeast Thai, Vietnamese and Cambodian neighbours. 'Khao niao', or sticky rice, is Laos's staple food and is eaten with every meal. It is eaten in numerous different ways, such as shaped into balls, ground and toasted, made into sweet cakes, or ground to bind sausages. Lao cuisine incorporates fresh vegetables and tropical fruits, meats and spices. Galangal, lemongrass, and padaek (fermented fish sauce) are important ingredients. Dishes are traditionally grilled, boiled, stewed, steamed, seared or mixed in salads. Stir-frying is now common but is considered to be of Chinese influence.

Mealtime is important in Laos. Traditionally, eating is communal, with diners sitting on a reed mat on the wooden floor around a raised platform woven out of rattan called a 'ka toke'. Meals are eaten by hand, with spoons used for soup and chopsticks used for noodles.

Colonial Cuisine

Vientiane has several good French restaurants where baguettes and croissants are widely available, both reminders of the country's French colonial past.

Laos market selling fresh baguettes

ON THE MENU

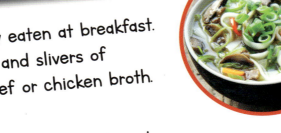

Phor is a noodle soup mainly eaten at breakfast. It consists of noodles, onions and slivers of chicken, pork or beef, in a beef or chicken broth.

Larb/Laap is a salad made from minced meat (raw or cooked) accompanied by a diverse assortment of vegetables, young leaves, herbs, seasoning and spice.

Sai Oua, Sai Gok lao-style pork sausages are essential to many Lao dishes. The pork is mixed with galangal, kaffir leaves, shallots, lemongrass, coriander, chillies and fish sauce. Some include sticky rice inside.

Khao Piak Sen this chewy noodle soup is made with rice noodles, pork or chicken, lemongrass, galangal, shallots, garlic, chopped coriander leaves, bean sprouts and slow cooked in bone broth and served with freshly sliced limes. It is considered to be a comfort food.

Mok Pa (Steamed fish in banana leaves) is fish cooked with lemongrass, kaffir lime leaves, fish sauce and chillies, and then wrapped up and steamed.

GEOGRAPHY AND CLIMATE

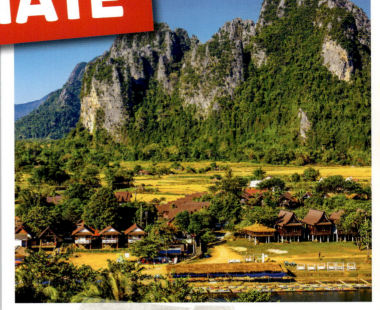

Laos covers 236,800 square kilometres and is located in the heart of Southeast Asia. It is landlocked with Vietnam, Cambodia, Myanmar, Thailand and China bordering it. It is a country with abundant natural resources and a wide variety of fauna and flora. Over 70 per cent of the country is mountainous.

Busy floating market on the Mekong River

River Life

The western border of Laos is marked by the Mekong River, which originates in the Yunnan Province of China and travels south, forming the boundary between Laos and its neighbours. The Mekong is vitally important to Laos. Almost all other rivers eventually feed into the Mekong and strongly affect Laotian daily life. These rivers provide a means of transport as well as providing fertile soils for agriculture.

Villages can flood during monsoon season

Climate

Laos's tropical climate is characterised by high temperatures and humidity throughout the year. April and May feature the hottest temperatures while the weather in June sees the monsoon pattern bringing heavy rain through to October. The climate varies by region, with cooler temperatures in the mountains in the north.

Top of the World
The country's highest peak is Phou Bia at 2,819 metres.

FABULOUS FLORA AND FAUNA

The rare Irrawaddy dolphin, 92 of these dolphins are estimated to still exist

Laos is well known for its rich variety of flora and fauna. There are over 20,000 species of plants in the Mekong area, 1,200 different kinds of bird and over 13,000 species of fish. The Mekong River is also home to the rare Irrawaddy dolphins.

Much of the country is covered by tropical and subtropical forest, and many species of flowering bamboo.

Laos has a number of animal species that are listed as vulnerable or critically endangered. These include the Asian Elephant, Banteng, black gibbon, red panda and tiger.

About 500 species of birds are in Laos, as well as many unique amphibians, reptiles and insects.

Some of the country's unusual animals are:

- Asiatic black bear
- Pileated gibbon
- Irrawaddy squirrel
- Asiatic golden cat

Pileated gibbon females have white fur whereas males have black fur

- Assamese macaque
- Buff-cheek gibbon
- Francois Leaf monkey
- Clouded leopard
- Long-tailed goral
- Sikkim rat
- Smooth-coated otter

The Asiatic golden cat is a medium-sized wild cat poached mainly for their fur

The grey long-trailed goral

MAJOR SITES

Tourism is growing annually, with more visitors discovering the natural wonders of Laos and its relaxed, welcoming people.

Luang Prabang

The town of Luang Prabang situated in northern Laos, was designated a UNESCO World Heritage Site in 1995. It was the ancient royal capital of the Lane Xang Kingdom and is still considered the heart of the country. This picturesque place is a mix of French colonial architecture, ancient temples and natural beauty. Located 700 metres above sea level and encircled by mountains, it is one of the country's most important tourism sites.

Important Sites

As of 2019, there are three UNESCO World Heritage sites in Laos. All three are World Cultural Heritage Sites and important tourist desitinations.

- Town of Luang Prabang
- Vat Phou and Associated Ancient Settlements within the Champasak Cultural Landscape
- Megalithic Jar Sites in Xiengkhuang – Plain of Jars

tourists visit the Plain of Jars historic site

28

Pha That Luang

The most sacred monument in Laos is Pha That Luang, or the Great Stupa. This gold-covered Buddhist stupa is in the centre of Vientiane and a place of great importance to the Laos people. Its image is also on the official seal of Laos.

Kuang Si Falls

The Kuang Si Falls, sometimes called Tat Kuang Si Waterfalls, is a three levelled waterfall about 29 kilometres south of Luang Prabang and one of the most beautiful natural wonders in Laos.

Other Major Sites
- Vientiane
- Vang Vieng
- Tad Fane Waterfall
- 4000 Islands region
- Kong Lor Cave
- Vat Phou

TRANSPORT

Laos is a landlocked country with no ports or sea harbours. The Mekong provides river travel opportunities but these can be long. Rail has only developed recently, with plans for a major rail line underway. There are several modes of transport that have been modernising in recent years, including highways and airports, but it will take some time to reach the standards of a developed country.

In cities, buses and trucks clog the highways. There are numerous bus companies that travel longer distances, while motorbikes and tuk tuks are used for shorter trips. Many people in rural areas still travel by foot, ox-cart or pack-horse.

Travelling by ox cart in rural Laos

Water Transport

Laos has about 4,587 kilometres of navigable water routes, primarily the Mekong and its tributaries. A further 3,000 kilometres of waterways is navigable to smaller boats.

FLAGS, SYMBOLS AND EMBLEMS

National Emblem

The emblem of Laos depicts the national shrine Pha That Luang. On each side are stalks of rice. The inscription on the bottom reads: "Peace, independence, democracy, unity and prosperity." The emblem was adopted in 1992.

Flag of Laos

The Laotian flag has a white circle on a blue field that is said to represent the moon shining over the Mekong River. The blue stripe represents wealth and the red represents the blood shed during the internal struggle for freedom. The Laos flag was officially adopted on December 2, 1975.

National Symbol

Indian elephant

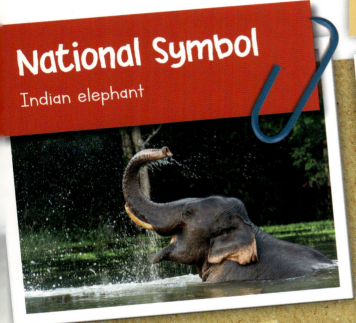

National Anthem

The national anthem of the Lao People's Democratic Republic is Pheng Xat Lao (literally "Hymn of the Lao People"). It was composed by Dr Thongdy Sounthonevichit and adopted as the national anthem in 1945.

National Flower

Plumeria (Frangipani)

National Instrument

The 'Khene', which is a mouth organ made up of several pieces of bamboo.

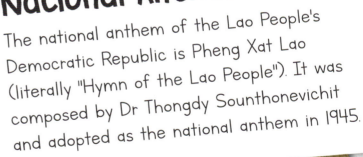

GLOSSARY

Baci	important Lao ceremonial custom
Buddhism	religion based on the teachings of Buddha
culture	practices, beliefs and customs of a society or people
endangered	when a species is at risk.
ethnic group	people who share a common culture, language and heritage
landmines	explosive traps that detonate when they are disturbed by a person or vehicle
Mekong River	trans-boundary river in Southeast Asia
monsoon	season of heavy rain
plateau	large, flat area found in higher regions
Stupa	mound-like structure or temple containing Buddhist relics
tropical	hot, humid climate

INDEX

climate 24-25, 32
clothes 13
cuisine 22
education 15
ethnic groups 10, 14
exports 7
fauna 24, 26
flag 31
flora 24, 26
geography 24
government 6-7, 10, 19-20
imports 7
landmines 8-9, 32
language 5, 14, 32
religion 5, 20, 32
sport 15
timeline 18-19
tourism 7, 9, 19, 28
transport 24, 30